ONLINE DATING
Solutions to Online Dating Problems

Juliet Edwin Carter

TABLE OF CONTENT

INTRODUCTION

Online dating has become a popular and convenient way for people to meet and connect with potential partners, but it can also present some challenges and potential problems. Some of the common issues that people may encounter while using online dating platforms include safety concerns, misrepresentation, and the time and effort required to create a profile and communicate with potential matches. While these issues can be frustrating and difficult to deal with, there are ways to address and solve them.

One solution to the issue of safety concerns is to be cautious and protect your personal information when using online dating sites and apps. This may involve using a pseudonym or screen name, rather than your real name, and being careful about sharing personal details with people you have only met online. It is also a good idea to meet in a public place for the first time, rather than at your home or the other person's home.

To address the issue of misrepresentation, it is important to be aware that not everyone may be who they say they are online. It can be helpful to be cautious and to try to verify information that people provide, such as by asking for additional photos or details about themselves. If you are considering meeting someone in person, it is a good idea to do some research to make sure they are who they claim to be.

To address the issue of time and effort, it may be helpful to set clear goals and priorities for your online dating experience. This may involve setting aside specific times to work on your profile or messaging potential matches and being mindful of how much time and effort you are putting into the process.

Finally, to address the issue of rejection, it is important to remember that not everyone you message or connect with online will be interested in you, and that is okay. It is important to keep an open mind and be open to meeting people who may not be a perfect match according to the platform's algorithms.

Overall, while online dating can present some challenges and potential problems, there are ways to address and solve these issues in order to have a positive and successful experience.

CHAPTER I

Defination of Online Dating

Online dating is the process of using the internet to connect with and communicate with potential romantic partners. It involves creating a profile on a dating website or app and using the platform to search for and communicate with other users who are also looking for relationships. Online dating can be a convenient and effective way to meet new people, particularly for those who may not have many opportunities to meet potential partners in their everyday lives. It can also be a useful tool for people who are interested in finding partners who share specific interests or characteristics. Online dating platforms use various methods, such as matching algorithms and user-provided information, to help users find and connect with potential partners.

Popularity of Online Dating

Online dating has become increasingly popular in recent years, as more and more people have turned to the internet to connect with and communicate with potential romantic partners. According to a survey conducted by the Pew Research Center in 2019, around 39% of American adults had used an online dating site or app at some point in their lives. The popularity of online dating has been driven in part by the increasing use of the internet and the proliferation of dating apps, as well as by the convenience and accessibility of these platforms. Online dating can be especially appealing to people who may not have many opportunities to meet potential partners in their everyday lives, or who are interested in finding partners who share specific interests or characteristics.

Purpose of the Book

There are many reasons why someone might write a book on online dating problems and their possible solutions. Some possible motivations for writing this particular book might include:

- To help people who are using online dating platforms and experiencing problems or challenges
- To provide information and guidance to people who are new to online dating and are unsure how to navigate the process
- To offer strategies and tips for overcoming common issues that can

arise when using online dating sites and apps
- To address the growing popularity of online dating and the need for resources and support for people who are using these platforms
- To contribute to the body of knowledge and understanding about online dating and the challenges and solutions that are associated with it

Overall, this book could be a valuable resource for people who are interested in using online dating platforms and want to have a positive and successful experience.

Common Problems of Online Dating

There are several frequent concerns that individuals may experience when utilizing online dating services. Some of these difficulties include:

- Safety concerns: Meeting someone online, especially if you have never seen them in person before, might be perilous. It is crucial to be careful and secure your personal information while utilizing online dating services and applications.

- Misrepresentation: People may not always be who they claim they are online. It is crucial to be aware of this potential and to be careful when chatting with someone you meet online, particularly if you are contemplating seeing them in person.
- Time and effort: Online dating may be time-consuming, since you may need to devote a substantial amount of time and effort to building a profile, contacting people, and going on dates.
- Rejection: Rejection is a common part of the dating experience, but it may be particularly tough to cope with when it happens online. It is crucial to understand that not everyone you

contact or interact with online will be interested in you, and that is alright.

- Matching algorithms: Some online dating services utilize algorithms to recommend prospective matches for you, however, these algorithms may not always be accurate or helpful. It is crucial to retain an open mind and be open to meeting individuals who may not be a great match according to the platform's algorithms.
- Communication issues: It may be difficult to successfully communicate with individuals you have just met online, and misunderstandings or miscommunications can arise. It is crucial to be clear and straightforward in your communication and to be open to addressing any misconceptions that may develop.
- Scams and fraudulent activity: Unfortunately, some individuals utilize

online dating sites to attempt to swindle or defraud others. It is crucial to be aware of this potential and to be careful when communicating with individuals you meet online.

Overall, internet dating may provide several obstacles and potential issues, but with careful preparation and an emphasis on safety and communication, it is possible to have a happy and successful experience.

CHAPTER II

Some Problems With Online Dating Site

There are some frequent concerns that users may experience while utilizing online dating services:

- Catfishing: Some individuals build phony accounts or use someone else's images to mislead others.
- Lack of authenticity: It might be tough to identify whether the person you are speaking with is being real or not.
- Safety concerns: There is always the possibility of harm when meeting someone in person who you have only met online.
- Inequality and discrimination: Some individuals may suffer prejudice based on their color, gender, age, or other

criteria while utilizing online dating services.

- Ghosting: This is when someone abruptly stops replying to your communications without any explanation. It may be annoying and painful.
- Misalignment of expectations: It may be difficult to identify what someone else is looking for in a relationship, and this can lead to misunderstandings or disappointment.
- Time and effort: Finding a suitable match might take a lot of time and effort, and it may not always be successful.
- Scams & fraud: Some persons utilize internet dating as a technique to swindle others out of money or personal information.

Unfortunately, internet dating scams and fraud are widespread occurrences. Scammers may use online dating services and apps to attempt to deceive users into giving them money or personal information. These scams may take various forms, such as asking for money to aid with a medical emergency or pretending to be a service member posted abroad who needs financial support.

Overall, it is necessary to be careful and aware of these possible risks while utilizing online dating services.

Safety Concern

Meeting someone in person who you have only met online might be perilous since you don't know the individual's genuine intentions or history. It is crucial to be careful and take efforts to safeguard your safety while utilizing online dating services.

Misrepresentation and Unrealistic Expectations

It is fairly unusual for individuals to misrepresent themselves or have unreasonable expectations while utilizing online dating services. Some individuals may construct phony accounts or use outdated or inaccurate images, while others may misrepresent their interests or achievements in their profiles. This might lead to disappointment or misunderstandings when you meet in person.

Unrealistic expectations may also be an issue in online dating. Some individuals may have a definite sense of what they are seeking for in a mate, and they may have difficulties finding someone who fulfills those expectations. This might lead to dissatisfaction and disappointment.

Difficulty Finding a Compatible Match

Finding a good match may be tough for many individuals who utilize online dating services. There are a lot of reasons that might contribute to this issue, such as:

- Limited pool of prospective matches: Depending on your area and the dating service or app you are using, you may have a somewhat narrow pool of potential mates to pick from.

- Misalignment of values and objectives: It might be difficult to assess if you and a possible match have comparable values and ambitions, and this can lead to misunderstandings or disappointment.
- Different communication styles: Different individuals have different communication styles, and this may lead to misunderstandings or trouble developing a relationship.
- Time and effort: Finding a suitable match might take a lot of time and effort, and it may not always be successful.

To maximize your chances of finding a suitable match, it is crucial, to be honest, and real in your online dating profile and to speak freely and honestly with possible matches. It is also a good idea to be open-minded and to explore trying multiple dating sites or apps to discover which one works best for you. Finally, it is crucial to be patient and to have an open mind, since it may take time to locate the ideal individual.

Solutions to Online Dating Problems

Here are some answers to the main challenges that individuals may experience while utilizing online dating services:

- Catfishing: To prevent being tricked by bogus profiles, it is vital to be vigilant and to conduct some research on the person's profile, including checking their social media accounts and doing a reverse image search on their profile picture. If you feel that a profile is false, you should report it to the dating site or app.
- Lack of authenticity: To prevent being duped by someone who is not being real, it is vital to talk freely and

honestly with possible matches and to be skeptical of anybody who appears too good to be true.

- Safety concerns: To ensure your safety when meeting someone in person who you have only met online, it is crucial to follow safety advice such as meeting in a public location, alerting a friend or family member where you are going, and having an evacuation plan.
- Inequality and discrimination: To prevent suffering prejudice based on your ethnicity, gender, age, or other variables, it is crucial to choose dating services or apps that have rules in place to combat inequality and discrimination.
- Ghosting: To prevent getting ghosted, it is crucial to talk freely and honestly with prospective matches about your expectations and limits.

- Misalignment of expectations: To prevent misunderstandings or disappointment, it is crucial, to be honest, and sincere in your online dating profile and to speak freely and honestly with possible matches about your beliefs and aspirations.
- Time and effort: To maximize your chances of finding a suitable match, it is a good idea to be open-minded and explore trying other dating services or apps. It is also crucial to be patient and to have an open mind, since it may take time to locate the ideal individual.
- Scams and fraud: To protect yourself against online dating scams, it is vital to be vigilant and to avoid transferring money or personal information to someone you have just met online. You should also be skeptical of profiles that look too good to be true or that have very little information, and you should

conduct some research on the person's page. If you feel that you are being scammed, you should cease speaking with the individual and report them to the dating site or app. You could also consider calling police enforcement or the Federal Trade Commission to report the fraud.

CHAPTER III

Conclusion

In conclusion, internet dating may be a valuable tool for those who are searching for a romantic connection, but it is vital to be aware of the possible difficulties that might occur. Some prevalent difficulties include catfishing, lack of authenticity, safety concerns, inequity and discrimination, ghosting, misalignment of expectations, time and effort, and scams and fraud. To protect yourself and maximize your chances of finding a good match, it is necessary to be careful, honest, and open-minded while utilizing online dating services. By following these recommendations and being aware of the possible pitfalls, you may have a pleasant experience with online dating.

Recap to the Main Problems and Solutions to Online Dating

Here is a list of the key difficulties and solutions in online dating:

Problems:

- Catfishing: People create phony accounts or utilize someone else's images to mislead others.
- Lack of authenticity: It might be tough to identify whether the person you are speaking with is being real or not.
- Safety concerns: There is always the possibility of harm when meeting someone in person who you have only met online.
- Inequality and discrimination: Some individuals may suffer prejudice based on their color, gender, age, or other criteria while utilizing online dating services.

- Ghosting: This is when someone abruptly stops replying to your communications without any explanation.
- Misalignment of expectations: It may be difficult to know what someone else is looking for in a relationship, which can lead to misunderstandings or disappointment.
- Time and effort: Finding a suitable match might take a lot of time and effort, and it may not always be successful.
- Scams & fraud: Some individuals use internet dating as a tool to swindle others out of money or personal information.

Solutions:

- To prevent being duped by phony profiles, it is vital to be vigilant and to conduct some research on the person's profile, including verifying their social media accounts and doing a reverse image search on their profile picture. If you feel that a profile is false, you should report it to the dating site or app.

- To prevent being duped by someone who is not being genuine, it is necessary to talk freely and honestly with possible mates and to be skeptical of anybody who appears too good to be true.
- To safeguard your safety when meeting someone in person who you have only met online, it is crucial to follow safety recommendations such as meeting in a public area, alerting a friend or family member where you are going, and having an evacuation plan.
- To prevent suffering prejudice based on your ethnicity, gender, age, or other variables, it is crucial to choose dating

services or apps that have rules in place to combat inequality and discrimination.

- To prevent getting ghosted, it is crucial to talk freely and honestly with prospective matches about your expectations and limits.
- To prevent misunderstandings or disappointment, it is crucial, to be honest, and true in your online dating profile and to talk freely and honestly with possible matches about your beliefs and ambitions.
- To maximize your chances of finding a suitable match, it is a good idea to be open-minded and explore trying multiple dating services or apps. It is also crucial to be patient and to have an open mind, since it may take time to locate the ideal individual.
- To protect yourself against online dating scams, it is necessary to be

vigilant and avoid transferring money or personal information to someone you have just met online. You should also be skeptical of profiles that look too good to be true or that have very little information, and you should conduct some research on the person's page. If you feel that you are being scammed, you should cease speaking with the individual and report them to the dating site or app. You could also consider calling police enforcement or the Federal Trade Commission to report the fraud.

The Importance of Being Aware and Proactive in Online Dating

It is crucial to be alert and proactive while utilizing online dating services to protect yourself and have a great experience. This includes being aware of phony profiles and frauds, interacting freely and honestly with prospective matches, and following safety recommendations when meeting someone in person.

By being aware of the various difficulties that might occur and taking action to protect yourself, you can boost your chances of finding a good match and having a great experience with online dating. It is also crucial to be open-minded and have an open mind, since it may take time to locate the ideal individual.

Ultimately, the key to having a successful and good experience with online dating is to be aware of the various difficulties that might occur and to take proactive actions to protect yourself and find a suitable match. So, it is crucial to be cautious and take the required safeguards when utilizing online dating services.

Future Development and Trend in Online Dating

There are a lot of trends and advancements in online dating that are expected to continue in the future. Some of them include:

- Increased usage of artificial intelligence and machine learning: Dating apps and services are anticipated to continue to employ AI and machine learning to enhance the matching process and deliver more tailored suggestions to users.

- Increased attention to user safety: With the increased awareness of online safety issues, dating apps and sites are expected to continue to concentrate on adding safeguards to protect users from scams and fraud.

- Greater connection with social media: It is conceivable that dating apps and sites may become more tightly connected with social media platforms, enabling users to share more information and interact with their social networks.

- Continuous expansion of niche dating sites and apps: There is expected to be a continued rise in the number of niche dating sites and apps that cater to certain hobbies or demographics.

- Increased usage of video and live streaming: With the advent of video and live streaming technologies, it is expected that dating apps and sites will integrate more video and live streaming capabilities in the future.

- Greater usage of virtual and augmented reality: Virtual and augmented reality technology might be utilized in the future to provide immersive dating experiences or to enable individuals to virtually "meet" and engage with each other.

Overall, the future of online dating is likely to be determined by developments in technology and a sustained emphasis on user safety and personalization.

www.ingramcontent.com/pod-product-compliance
Lightning Source LLC
LaVergne TN
LVHW052113160826
845678LV00015B/3530

* 9 7 9 8 3 7 1 5 5 2 4 2 6 *